ADVERSITY TO ADVENTURE:

HOW TO CONNECT THE DOTS WHEN THE UNEXPECTED HAPPENS

FUNMI AKINSANYA-ALAKE

ENDORSEMENTS

Adversity to Adventure is a masterpiece, a timeless gold and a recapitulation of the excellent steps needed to weather the storms embedded in the journey of life. The reference material serves as an engine room for transformation from obscurity to relevance.

Adversity to Adventure is robust in interpretation, congruent in approach and fertile for positive thinking. It provides an intellectual platform on the strategic areas of life. Everyone goes through adversity but not everyone knows how to benefit from it. Adversity is a transitional experience and not a paralytic exercise. This book is a tonic for boosting your capacity for success.

It is a world class publication.

Adversity to Adventure is balanced in scope, succinct in content and lucid in presentation. The pragmatic life experiences shared in this book will propel you to success irrespective of environmental and inherent limitations

I am convinced beyond any contradiction to recommend this book to you because it is designed and structured to move you to the next level of significance and success. I hereby endorse this book. Happy reading!

PROF (AMB) ADETUNJI ADEFUNMILAYO HAASTRUP

Wisconsin Professor of Management, Global Ambassador of Leadership Development of Mogul, New York USA; Member of United Nations Foundation, Washington USA; Member of Harvard University's Business Review Council, Massachusetts USA and Fellow of the Prestigious International Academy of Management, UK

Funmi Alake, aka "Lady Shabach", is a delightful, highly motivated community activist, full of energy and determination to succeed. Having known her for many years and her drive to impact and empower people with disability and other women in our community is worthy of note and this was the drive and determination that led us to form Cutting Edge Community Forum (CECF) in 2017.

Something I do for inspiration is to look for people who have overcome adversity because it gives me hope that I can do the same. Although I love analysing people and how they accomplished what they did, it'd be a lot easier if there was some formula. Funmi Alake provides just that in her new book - Adversity to Adventure. I am endorsing the book, after having read it. And if you are like me, your message will be, "Bring it on, life!"

It's not over until you WIN. Imagine if Funmi had not let go of her past - forgetting the pain of being made redundant from a thriving career path of over 10 years. She wasn't calling a pity party of friends but instead she saw a new horizon and changed her line of questioning from "Why me?" to "What next?" - choosing to turn her adversity to an adventure.

This book is about Funmi's journey through redundancy and the endless opportunities that opened up for her to explore her untapped potentials. How do you prepare for a sudden change of life? To quote from the book, "Life happens, and it can happen to the best of us". How we deal with life at that point is what makes us unique or distinct. The book talks about the different seasons of life and how, with God's help, we can navigate through gloriously.

The book emphasises the power of prayer when going through adversity and it says "You cannot wish away an adversity but you can pray about it, make the most of it and grow through it." I particularly love the spirit oozing out of her when she says "One of the best ways to push through adversity is to learn to laugh at yourself. Do not take yourself too seriously and be miserable."

Indeed, it's impossible to finish this book without believing that regardless of your circumstances, you have the power to succeed in a world that keeps trying to knock you off your path. I wholeheartedly endorse this book and recommend it to all who are interested in their continuous advancement. I am very excited about the dynamic change this book will make in the lives of those who read it.

Councillor Afolasade Bright - Former Civic Mayor of London Borough of Hackney

Cabinet Member for Employment, Skills & Aspirations, London Borough of Barking & Dagenham

I cannot imagine how challenging it would have been to distil the experiences of overcoming adversity, but I do know that Funmi did it with a finesse which only a talented author like herself possibly could. With an unapologetically realistic delivery packed with emotion, Adversity to Adventure is a crucially important portrayal of how we deal with those inevitable challenging periods of our lives that will ultimately determine whether we remain a victim or emerge victorious. If you have ever wondered how to connect the dots that transport you to your destiny, then this is an unflinchingly honest place to start.

Councillor Sanchia Alasia

Former Mayor of the London Borough of Barking and Dagenham

DEDICATION

This book is dedicated to all those who have been battered and bruised in the face of adversity.

To those who have overcome; congratulations for not staying defeated

To those who are yet to overcome; It's not over yet, your joy is coming in the morning.

ACKNOWLEDGEMENTS

I am eternally grateful to my Father in Heaven for his steadfast love that never ceases, his mercies that never come to an end. So great is His faithfulness.

Now to the King eternal, immortal, invisible, to God who alone is wise, be honour and glory forever and ever. Amen.

To all the beautiful people who were part of my journey from Adversity to Adventure, nothing but love for you. THANK YOU.

CONTENTS

FOREWORD

Adversity, like any other issue of life, connotes different things to different people, depending on its intensity, duration and of course the capacity, experience and maturity of the individual going through it. Adversity takes different levels and can leave a permanent scar, if wrongly handled. This is the driving force behind the publishing of this book: Adversity to Adventure by Funmi Akinsanya-Alake. It is based on her personal experience and the main objective is to give a balanced picture on the reality of adversity. Also, this book is unique because, apart from being an easy read, it contains principles, precepts, and revelations to empower, motivate and change your life. Equally, paying attention to the noteworthy and significant essentials within these pages guarantees that your life will never be the same in Jesus' name.

Funmi's tenacity and doggedness shine through this book from the very first page to the last without any reservation. I am delighted to have been asked to write the forward this book.

Pastor Gbolahan Bright, MBE

RCCG The Master's Sanctuary, London UK

PREFACE

Wait! I didn't get the memo.

Have I really just been made redundant? Oh, no! I didn't see that coming. I love my job and have been working in the same organisation for a little over ten years. Why should they let me go now? I have consistent excellent appraisals, and I have no issues whatsoever with my boss or any colleague. I have settled so comfortably into this work family. In fact, I brought in some of my own family and friends to work part-time during the holiday, and they had nothing but love for this organisation.

It was initially supposed to be a two-week contract as a customer service officer, to cover for someone who was on annual leave. However, just before the two weeks elapsed, another lady was going on maternity leave. Then my contract was renewed, and it so happened that I continued in the role for another two years. The two years soon rolled into ten years plus within the same organisation, working in different capacities. From customer service officer to finance officer to management accountant and then financial accountant. I mean, I saw nothing but God's hands. It was a seamless transition into each of those roles. I yearned for them and worked hard to attain those heights.

My love and commitment blossomed for the fact that the organisation's ethos was built on core values that aligned with mine, and that they were big on making a social impact. And the salary at the time was perfect for me. What more could a girl want? It seemed like I was now reaching the pinnacle of my career. In fact, the year prior to being made redundant, I had received an employee appreciation award in recognition of ten years of excellent service.

And now, have I just been told that sentence every employee dread to hear, "Sorry, we have to let you go"? Seriously, there must be a mistake somewhere. I guess you know the sort of questions that come straight to mind when things like this happen. *Is God setting me up or what? Why Me?*

I have heard people ask these questions time and time again in times of adversity. And rightly so. How do you prepare for a sudden change in life? What do you do when people you have trusted in disappoint you, or the things you have built your hopes on collapse? How do you begin a new vocation or develop a new skill set when you have put in a lifetime of dedication, commitment and hard work to a chosen career or business? What do you do when a relationship you have invested so much in is falling apart in the twinkle of an eye?

When institutions that you expected to protect you suddenly pull the rug from under your feet, how do you bounce back? What do you do if you have tried to get back into work but there are no job offers? If you are the breadwinner of your family, what do you say to them when you are faced with the reality that you may not be able to fulfil your obligations any longer? What could be going on in your mind when every sense of personal accomplishment and pride is stripped off you? Can you dare to face a family that you practically abandoned in order to pursue your dream business or career, when after all that, it seems your world has fallen apart? Where do you go when the people you consult for help, also need help themselves?

These and many other questions go through our minds when we find ourselves in situations that we do not have control over; situations that are unexpected or unpreventable. The fact is that we must come to an understanding that life happens, and it can happen to the best of us.

I write this book to share with you some of the principles that helped me in my journey through redundancy and how the experience has opened the opportunity for me to explore my untapped creativity. I dare say that so many things I have done post-redundancy, including writing this book, might not have been accomplished if I had remained in my previous role.

As you read this book, you will begin to view times of transition and adversity from a new perspective, such that your question will change from "Why me?" to "What next?"

I share with you how I chose to turn my **adversity** into an **adventure**.

I trust that by the time you finish reading the pages ahead, you will be bold to embrace the next season of your life, and allow new possibilities to lead you to the paths of discovering your purpose and fulfilling your potential.

CHAPTER 1

CHANGE IS A GIVEN, REACTION IS OPTIONAL

"Change is the law of life. And those who look only to the past or present are certain to miss the future."

- John F. Kennedy

C hange is the only constant thing in this world. Its inevitability is such that everyone on the face of the earth will have to go through it at one point or the other. Life is always moving forward, and nothing ever remains the same. Our lives are in a constant state of transition.

Just as seasons change, so do people. It is not everyone that you meet in your life's journey that will stay with you throughout. There are those who will travel with you and stay a lifetime, whereas some you will only meet at crossroads. You gain some, you lose some. So, as people come into our lives for different purposes, things also happen to us for different purposes.

Life is like a book. There are good chapters and there are bad ones. You do not stop reading the book when you get to the bad chapters, because if you do, you will never know what happens next. The reality is that a lot of times we tend to close the book when we get to the seemingly bad or uninteresting part of the story. We do not follow through to see if there will be another good chapter ahead. We tend to give up and lose hope too easily. We assume that because of our background and disposition, some things are not permitted to happen to us, forgetting that we have no part in orchestrating our existence in life itself.

Personal Experience

Life does not always give us what we think we deserve. We cannot get what we want all the time; we cannot have somebody that we love all the time. I did not think life was fair to me when I had to go back to college at the age of forty-five to do an "Access to Nursing" course, considering that I already had a first and a postgraduate degree. I did not feel that I deserved to be made redundant. I also thought I would get a job almost immediately after redundancy, but that did not happen.

Because I needed to make ends meet, I settled for jobs that were beneath my qualifications. As if it was not bad enough that I earned about four times more per hour in my previous role than I did now, at one point, I couldn't get enough hours to make the pay add up to cover the bills. I did not feel like life was fair to make me start all over again after almost reaching the peak of my previous career. Every time I worked in those roles or stayed back at college to study, I sometimes paused to remember where I was coming from and it got clearer to me each time that life is not perfect.

However, despite its imperfections, life is beautiful, and we must see it as such. The fact is that we can never run away from problems, obstacles, or adversities. They are part of life and we must learn to find positive ways of navigating these circumstances. One of the reasons why there is a high rate of suicide and mental health disorders is that most people only focus on the ugly side of life. They keep their heads down in sorrow or regret, not knowing that the light of hope and a fresh new beginning is right in front of them.

When we fail to embrace the reality of change in our lives, we can become so disillusioned to the point that we are unable to manage the change positively and effectively. It must be admitted, though, that many factors could influence the way we approach and manage change. These include the intensity of the change, the resulting effect, and the severity of the impact on our lives. Most people can deal with change when it is gradual but will break down when faced with a sudden or dramatic change.

Man is a creature of habit. We feel irritated and disgruntled when change occurs. And rightly so, because we are so accustomed to our ways of doing things and we are not prepared for the time it will take to adjust to this new circumstance or reality that has come to shake up our stability.

Mastering Change

In his book, *The Principles and Benefits of Change*, the late Dr Myles Munroe highlighted four types of changes we experience in life thus:

1). Change that happens to us - either anticipated or unexpected - that can affect our personal lives, careers, and families. An example of this is being made redundant, losing a loved one, or going through a relationship breakup. This can lead to financial difficulties, mental stress, or emotional breakdown.

2). Change that happens around us. This type of change affects our community, nation, or the world at large. An obvious example is the current COVID-19 pandemic, which has facilitated a new normal, and the way we do life generally. It has disrupted the economy of nations and convulsed thousands of businesses worldwide.

3). Change that happens within us. This change can directly affect us physically, emotionally, mentally, or spiritually. A sudden illness will alter a person's daily life and could mean they are dependent on others for support in meeting basic needs. A person with a mental health illness - resulting in depression, excessive outbursts, or regular frustration - could face the risk of a weakened immune system and other serious diseases.

4). Change that we initiate. This is a planned change. A person can say to himself or herself, "I am tired of this job I am doing; I need to apply for a better one." Or "I would love to live in a particular part of the town or city." To achieve this, they begin to go through the process of making this change happen, and then implement the plans that will move them from the present state to a preferred future.

The reality is that most changes that we go through are not always initiated by us, otherwise the impact on us would not be as adverse as it is often experienced. However, it is our approach to change that largely determines whether it will work for or against us.

Think about it. How do you approach change? Are you proactive or reactive? When we are proactive to change, we plan, taking into consideration potential problems and how to handle them should they arise. On the other hand, being reactive is when there is no plan or strategy in place for when a problem arises, thus causing us to have a negative attitude towards the change.

Even when there are plans and strategies in place, what we should be doing is responding to change, and not reacting. When we respond, we take charge of the situation, whereas when we react, change could ultimately become a burden.

Downsides of Being Reactive

More specifically, a reactive approach to change will cause any of the following to happen:

You can become angry at change. Yes, you have probably experienced this at one point or another in your life. You were so angry at what happened because you felt you did not deserve it. You believed you had dotted all the i's and crossed all the t's, so things should at least go as near perfect as planned, if not perfect. You had it in your subconscious somewhere that certain things only happened to certain people, not people like you. If you are a born-again, Spirit-filled child of God, I'm sure you must have claimed and declared, "That is not my portion." Why then should that be happening to you without at least forewarning you, so you could properly prepare to deal with it? Well, the Scripture has prepared you. Psalm 34:19, for instance, says: "Many are the afflictions of the righteous, But the Lord delivers him out of them all." The thing about anger is that it is a spirit that can poison one's thoughts thereby causing one to behave irrationally and making self-destructive decisions. A man who is given to anger can destroy, in a minute, what has taken him many years to build. No wonder the Scripture says in Ecclesiastes 7:9, "Do not hasten in your spirit to be angry, For anger rests in the bosom of fools." Being angry at unfavourable circumstances often comes with a lot of consequences. Anger leads to bitterness, which will eat you up physically, emotionally, and even spiritually. If care is not taken, you can develop internal stress, which can lead to physical illness. Moreover, there is a high tendency of playing the blame game – that is, accusing others of being responsible for your 'misfortune'. You begin to verbally attack friends, family or even become antagonistic to the society in general. Also, in a bid to angrily resist change, you may begin to take up unhealthy or destructive practices. These include binge eating/drinking, oversleeping, and getting addicted to television or social media. Trust me, anger will not make things better; rather, it will cost you, big time.

1. You can simply accept change.

When life strikes a blow, some people simply get stuck in the aftermath. They acknowledge that change is coming or is already happening but do nothing about it, even when their indifference is obviously detrimental to their progress.

Suppose, for instance, that your car's dashboard has been flashing "service due". That is a warning that you need to take that car for service soon. If you decide to continue using it and ignore the warnings, you know what the repercussions will be. You cannot merely accept that the car needs service; you need to take it to the garage for service.

Think about instances where you simply gave in to situations that you were well able to do something about. I'm sure you are not happy about the eventual outcome. When you stop at merely accepting change, you will become a victim of the change. You do not accept changes that do not align with your values.

The reason you see people starting petitions to the government or authorities in their countries is to call for certain measures to be put in place that they know may affect them or even others. They do not just stand and say, "Oh well, since the government or the authorities in place have said it, so be it." You will notice that people who just accept anything that happens to them never experience a transformed life. For them, anything goes. I'm sure that's not you. Well, I do not want that to be you!

2. You can accommodate or adjust to change.

An interesting incident came to mind as I write this, and I always laugh whenever I remember it. When I came over to the UK from Nigeria to do my postgraduate studies, my first stop on arrival was with family friends for a few nights, until my rented accommodation was sorted.

When I finally arrived at this accommodation owned by a lovely family, the daughter of the landlady showed me to my room. As the door swung open (well, barely), I looked inside and thought, "Oh, this must be the room to put my suitcase and bags." But I soon realised it was my room. The box room was where I would be staying for the next one year and six months! This box room had a single bed, a two-door wardrobe, and a desk and chair. I was not sure how to react, but I put on a fake smile and dropped my stuff. I am not one to complain but I knew that I was going to express my disappointment somehow.

Now, you have to understand what the problem was. I had just left behind, in Africa, a large en-suite room with a king-sized bed, and here I was in London, for which I had nurtured high expectations, now having to make do with this box room. I had not been involved in the search for the accommodation, as everything had been sorted out for me prior to my arrival.

Next day, I rang home, and I narrated the situation (kind of complained) to my dad. As is characteristic of him, he joked, "Young lady, do you want us to send your bed from here? That is what I keep telling you people (in a typical Nigerian dad's style). You never know where you will end up; you have to appreciate what you have." And then he started laughing.... just imagine! That was not even remotely funny.

Oh well, eventually, I kind of laughed at myself too. My dad had paid for my studies and accommodation; so, the least I could do was to be grateful for what I had and make the best of it. Once I found my feet in the UK, then I could make the changes I so desired.

I am sure this is a common situation that a lot of people face when they arrive in a new city or country. Suffice it to say that I adjusted to this new environment for the time I stayed there, even though I had to alter a few things in my schedule to help me adapt. I was lucky enough to have a very lovely hostess and family; so, I used their kitchen to entertain friends when they came visiting.

3. **You can become a victim of change**.

When you become angry at change, or live in denial, this can result in becoming a victim of change. Once you do not find a way to positively interact with change, you are prone to becoming a by-product of its effects. You become a victim when certain changes are taking place around you and you refuse to do nothing about them.

Consider, for instance, the issue of the recent pandemic that the whole world is facing. There are restrictions to physical meetings or gatherings in large groups; and as such most organisations have had to find alternative ways of carrying out their businesses. Because most interactions and transactions are now done virtually, it is imperative for us to be equipped with skills that will enable us to be technology savvy, to keep up with the current trend. Religious institutions that were already streaming on social media platforms are basically just continuing to do what they've always done, except for meeting together at a location. Those who had been against using social media platforms as a tool of reaching out have become victims of this change.

4. **You can deny or ignore change**.

It is sometimes exceedingly difficult to accept the reality of an adverse situation. Some people find it difficult and unbearable to come to terms with a loss or a catastrophic event. When change threatens our comfort and security, the tendency is for us to retreat into a world of denial. The truth, however, is that when changes like this occur, we cannot pretend that they are not happening.

Continuing business as usual when it is no longer usual can have a detrimental effect on your wellbeing. You need to give the change the place it deserves in the overall scheme of things. You need to deal with what has happened. This may well take time, but it is better than denying it. Seek to understand it, come to accept its reality, and then commit to fulfilling the new role it demands from you.

5. Make Change Work for You

Indeed, the onus is on each of us to decide what we do with change. Decide to be responsive to change rather than being reactive. But this must come after doing your due diligence of being proactive.

Since life involves a series of continuous transitions, we must always be prepared to respond to change in a way that will benefit us. The ability to respond, rather than react, puts you in control and reduces change to your servant.

If you react, change leads your life; if you respond, you lead change in your life.

Change moves us closer to God's purposes for our lives - if we allow it to. As bestselling author, Brian Tracy, advises, *"Resolve to be a master of change rather than a victim of change."*

CHAPTER 2

UNDERSTANDING YOUR SEASONS

"I believe in process. I believe in four seasons. I believe that winter's tough, but spring's coming. I believe that there's a growing season. And I think that if you realise that in life, you grow. You get better."

- Steve Southerland

There are different seasons in life. Seasons come and seasons go. Nothing ever stands still; nothing ever maintains its current state, identity, or shape for an exceptionally long time. When we take the time to reflect upon the natural environment, we begin to observe a complex yet incredibly beautiful world cycling through patterns, phases, and stages of transition.

Transformation is a natural part of life and an important component of human evolution. It is something that is unavoidable but very manageable. Our circumstances, needs, desires and behaviours must, therefore, naturally change and evolve alongside these cycles of life, or we risk undermining our personal levels of happiness and fulfilment.

Just as the earth experiences spring, then summer, then fall, and finally winter — your own life cycle has its seasons. And just as we experience these natural life cycles, we also experience spiritual life cycles. Think about when you told someone about a situation that you were going through, and their response to you was, "It's just a season, this too shall pass". You might have been convinced they had no clue! "How could what I am experiencing be just a season? If only they understood how long this has been going on for, they would understand that it cannot be 'just a season'!"

Echoes from Nature

The truth is our spiritual seasons typically mirror what we see in nature. There are similarities in both, as we will be examining shortly. This, however, does not mean that the specific pattern and timing of the seasons of our lives are exactly the same as those of nature. In other words, you cannot say because winter starts in December and ends in March, your winter season must follow that pattern. Still, God provides examples in the natural to help us understand our spiritual seasons. As Ecclesiastes 3:1 clearly states, "To everything there is a season, a time for every purpose under heaven."

Let's examine the different types of seasons there are and how to identify the season you may be in:

- **Fall**

If you look at nature, this is typically a time of things falling away. This is when we see the temperature and leaves begin to change, which is how we know that fall is coming.

It is also possible that, currently in your life, God is causing some things to fall away. What is He calling you to let go of? Nature provides a great example of how this should look in our life. Yet, more often than not, we want to hold on and not let go of things that could potentially cause problems in our next season.

Spiritual fall is a good time for you to grow your trust in God.

- **Winter**

Naturally, when we think of winter we think of rest. This is typically a time when things are not growing or blooming outside. Many animals are also hibernating (resting). If we are discerning, we can take a cue from nature when God calls us into a spiritual winter. We should not resist the rest. Rather, we should welcome the opportunity to recharge! This is a good time to really hear from God on direction and next steps.

Pray and journal during this season. Ideas typically will abound if you are getting proper rest during a spiritual winter. You may feel restless or unsure because it is not the time to harvest or act on the ideas. However, you can be strategic about planning and getting yourself set up for a bountiful spring. Take God up on His graciousness and rest in Him.

- **Spring**

We all love the fresh feelings spring brings! There is just this new zest for life and an unstoppable feeling when we are in a spiritual spring. This is the time that we are planting those ideas that may have come to us during our winter. It can also be the time to begin to see the early stages of blossoms and warmth, as our ideas begin to bloom, through our relationships and connections.

We are seeing God work on our behalf in our spiritual spring. This is a season that we typically do not have a hard time trusting Him.

- **Summer**

Who does not love summer? This is a time in the natural that we typically mix work with play. I recently read an article that pointed out the contrast of the heat and coolness you experience during the summer. So, although we are still diligently working, we should also be taking breaks so that we do not overheat.

How does this apply spiritually? This is the time to reap what you planted during your spiritual spring. It is a time to continue to work, while making sure to build refreshment and relaxation in as well. This is also a time for us to get rid of those "weeds" that may want to pop up and get us distracted. If we limit our distractions, a spiritual summer can be incredibly good for us.

Significance of Spiritual Seasons

I hope this helps you to pinpoint what spiritual season you are currently in. Once you have

a clear understanding of spiritual seasons, you will be able to make the most of each new season that God carries you through. You will also be able to trust Him more and increase your faith, as you see Him work on your behalf in each season.

As we go through the different seasons in our lives, it may sometimes feel like nothing new is happening; that there is no growth and no change in what we are going through. But that is not true! There is a purpose in our winters, just as there is in our summers! The fact that we cannot see or feel anything does not mean it is of no use.

There is a time to sow and there is a time to reap. God, in Genesis 8:22 declares, "While the earth remains, seedtime and harvest, cold and heat, winter and summer, and day and night shall not cease". The secret to contentment is to be okay with this order in which God has placed all things.

How do you handle your spiritual fall and winters? How can you begin to trust God more during a spiritual winter or fall - seasons that can be associated with periods of adversity, trouble or lack? During these times, we understand that our current life circumstances are only temporary, and we, therefore, make use of what we have to the best of our abilities.

On the other hand, when we resist these natural rhythms, we sell ourselves short and consequently struggle with the conditions that life throws our way. Certainly, if we approach life from a perspective of understanding that each season will teach us lessons on strength, endurance, growth, faith, and trust, we will conduct ourselves in a manner that will position us to reap maximum benefits from these periods.

Life is all about change. We are constantly changing, and our circumstances are simply a reflection of these natural evolutionary steps. The seasons of life are as temporary as the raindrops that are falling on your head, as the thunder that is raging outside, or as the wind that is blowing up the storm. None of these events will last forever. We must however note that our choices and the way we respond to any of these seasons will determine how long we remain in it.

The length of time it takes us to progress through each season is simply a reflection of our state of mind — a reflection of our ability to adapt to the conditions and circumstances we find ourselves in. If we adapt successfully, we will move through difficult and unpleasant phases quickly. On the other hand, if we are unable to adapt, then we bear the consequences of failing to capitalise on the opportunities that life inevitably throws our way.

The seasons of life are there to teach us lessons about ourselves, about others and about life in general. They are there to help us grow emotionally, physically, and spiritually. And they are there to nourish our soul, enliven our spirit and strengthen our emotional resilience in the face of adversity and opportunity.

Moreover, unlike the natural seasons which are fixed, the choices we make today could very well change the tide of our seasons as we move into tomorrow. This is why you must remain sensitive to the season you are in at every point in time. Be conscious of the different seasons you go through. It will help you to prepare and plan ahead.

When Seasons Revolve

Sometimes it feels like we are experiencing a recycle in the seasons we go through. You may feel like you have gone through a similar adversity, struggle, or trials before and that season should be over. But then comes another season of fall or winter – dark and gloomy, with things falling apart.

"Not again", you may say. But remember that we have these four seasons every calendar year. The strategy is to understand the purpose of God for you within that season. You may be going through the same season again because your assignment is changing, and you need to learn some lessons in that season to be able to effectively carry out that assignment.

When I had to go back to college because I needed to retrain so I could get a better job, I couldn't understand why I had to go through that season again, after having already attained a postgraduate degree level. I had been through the phase of passing through college at the age of eighteen, and here I was again at age forty-five, sitting with eighteen-year-olds and having to borrow my teenage daughter's biology textbook to assist with my studies.

Now, please note that it would have been a different ball game if it had been a conscious decision on my part as it were; but in this case, circumstances had led me back to a season where I had gone through as a teenager. I did not spend the time moaning about my circumstance. I made up my mind to embrace the phase, trusting that the purpose would be made manifest to me as time went on. And it was indeed made manifest. I realised that it prepared me for where God was taking me to and opened unimaginable doors unto me. I had no idea at the time, but I was intentional about enjoying the adventure. A lot of the skills that I have acquired were during the season of going back to college.

Since I started writing this book during the COVID-19 pandemic, let me use this season as an example. I am sure you know that the pandemic season will not last forever.

There have been similar seasons before and a possible similar season in the future. Now, even though the lockdown and the new normal are applicable to everyone worldwide, the irony is that we are not going through the same season individually. For the majority of people, it has been a season of loss of jobs, increase in unemployment rate, failing businesses, dwindling global economy and the likes. Yet, there are many others who are thriving in the same season. For some people, this is a time to learn new skills; for others, this is the time to put the skills that they have learnt before to use.

Personally, this season of the pandemic has been a time for me to retreat, unlearn and relearn. God has allowed me to use this period to also reset my priorities and be redirected to purpose. I had never accomplished so much in a few months as I did during the lockdown period. I have picked up keyboard playing skills and gained a certification as a life coach. I have had the opportunity to join amazing people that have contributed to my spiritual and personal growth, as well as receiving personal revelations for my purpose. And, of course, I started writing this book during the lockdown.

You must understand which season you are. Your season is not the same as somebody else's season. For you to enter your next season, you need to understand your present season. It may be that this is your season of preparation; it may be a season of reaping what you have sown previously; It may be a season for you to draw strength from God to prepare you for your next assignment.

Ask yourself, "Which season am I in?" Whatever season you find yourself in, embrace it and appreciate the unique gifts it has to offer. Whatever season you are going through, do not give up on your dreams and vision. Anyone can give up; it is the easiest thing to do. But to hold it together when everyone else would understand if you fell apart, that's true strength.

I trust that you will feel more encouraged that you are not alone in going through the different seasons of life. I am so glad that the Bible is clear about this subject, and that is where you should draw your strength from.

Ecclesiastes 3: 2-8 reveals:

"A time to be born, And a time to die;

A time to plant, And a time to pluck what is planted

A time to kill, And a time to heal;

A time to break down, And a time to build up;

A time to weep, And a time to laugh;

A time to mourn, And a time to dance;

A time to cast away stones, And a time to gather stones;

A time to embrace, And a time to refrain from embracing;

A time to gain, And a time to lose;

A time to keep, And a time to throw away

A time to tear, And a time to sew;

A time to keep silence, And a time to speak;

 A time to love, And a time to hate;

A time of war, And a time of peace".

"I have resolved to live, not just endure each season of my life"

CHAPTER 3

SEEKING THE ADVENTURE

"Only through experience of trial and suffering can the soul be strengthened, ambition inspired, and success achieved."

– Helen Keller

I stated earlier that nobody likes to go through adversity; but the fact remains that there are problems everywhere. I once heard the story of a lawyer who got up early one morning, and as he was preparing to leave home for the day, he received four long distance calls. Each one of the callers – or clients - had problems and they wanted him to come right away to help fix them. As he was still thinking about which to deal with first, he received two more calls - this time from clients who lived nearby. They also wanted him to come help fix their problems, and they wanted it right away.

Now more confused than ever, the lawyer could not be bothered about breakfast. He left the house and hailed a cab. Once inside the cab, the cab driver asked him where he would like to go, and the lawyer replied, "I do not care, I have got problems everywhere."

Have you tried to speak to friends or families about a problem you were facing, and they also began to share the problems that they were going through? Oh, now who is going to help who? If you are a human being, with the breath of life in you, you will encounter problems. You will face obstacles and adversities.

How you respond to adversity is what will either break you or make you. You cannot wish away adversity, but you can pray about it, make the most of it and grow through it.

Stings of Adversity

Back to my experience again. As more than a year rolled by after redundancy, and cash was not forthcoming, I found myself at the mercy of applying for benefits (jobseeker's allowance) at the job centre. I hated going to "sign on" every two weeks or so for money. Having worked so hard for fifteen years to get to where I got to, with God's favour backing me, I was now signing up for unemployment benefit. That was not my idea of progress.

I remember how I once went to "sign on" at the job centre and the adviser, a young guy of African descent, looked at me and said, "With all this experience of yours (looking at my CV), you should be employing people, not looking for employment." And to make light of the situation, he added, "Oh please remember me when you reach that level o; I might be needing a job." Then we both laughed, and I said a big "amen". Who wouldn't? Do I blame him? That was 2011. I had been on a £35k per annum salary and here I was signing on for £100 plus for a two-week allowance!

That was not even funny, but I had to laugh. From the part of the world where I come from, you would be asking yourself, *"Who did I offend?"*

So, my stint with the job centre lasted about three months. The process helps keep you in check as you have to keep a record of what you did to look for a job, the dates you searched for the roles, what happened after you searched and so on. I recall that when I filled an application form for a role then, one of the things expected to be put on the record sheet was "What I will do next". I would always fill in, "Awaiting outcome/Follow up application". And then these outcomes came back with "We regret to inform you that your skills do not match requirements", or sometimes I never got a reply. I was either overqualified or underqualified. Not a good place to be when you've always been in employment.

So, I told myself, "I think I've had enough of this. Jobseeker's allowance is a great idea, but for me, I'm done. It's time to move on."

And that was what I did. *I'm a celebrity, get me out of here! LOL*

Once I began to embrace my reality, I made a conscious decision that whatever my hands found to do, I would do it well, whether the role was beneath me or not. I decided I would seek to be adventurous and enjoy where I was on the way to where I desired to be.

Humour Yourself

One of the best ways to push through adversity is to learn to laugh at yourself. Do not take yourself too seriously and be miserable because life is happening to you. Proverbs 17:22 exhorts, "A merry heart does good like medicine, but a broken spirit dries the bones."

You have to tell yourself resolutely and consistently; *I am not going to allow this situation to deprive me of my joy. It is only but a phase, and this too shall pass.*

Laughter is truly the best medicine. It is your body's way of coping with stress, releasing tension and resetting your brain to be more positive. A good chuckle will release endorphins and dopamine, nature's feel-good chemicals.

It might seem unthinkable to find anything funny when you're struggling from one of life's blows. But sometimes just stepping back and seeing the humour of the situation can help lighten your mood and allow you to move forward. You may not be chuckling amid a major setback but give yourself some time. Finding your sense of humour when facing adversity is a healthy way to build resilience, no matter how bad your situation is. What I do in such instances is to share the situation with a few friends and laugh over it.

I knew that settling for receiving a jobseeker's allowance was just not it for me; but I had learnt something new that I would not have known if I had not been made redundant. I stopped looking for accounting roles and started to pursue my passion in event planning. I started to attend seminars and conferences on event planning. Then I went on to register with an event recruitment agency. I had the opportunity to work at some of London's big events, such as The Chelsea Flower Show, London Fashion Week, Excel's World Travel Market, and the likes.

While taking on these seasonal roles, I was also learning the tricks of the trade. I loved the way the exhibitions were organised, the professionalism and the way people from all over the world trooped to these events. It is still a life-long dream of mine to host an international exhibition that will attract thousands of visitors from all over the world.

My experiences working at these events spurred me on to start my own event outfit - Shabach Events - which has hosted two major networking and business exhibitions since inception. I was now growing; one of the gifts in me was blossoming. I did not stop at that but went on to enrol for an advanced diploma programme in Event Management and Communications. I loved every bit of it. I was beginning to change with the change. I was sure loving this adventure!

Keep Advancing – Against the Odds!

When I applied to do the Access to Nursing course at college, on the open day, I met with one of the tutors. I sat in front of her during the interview and she asked me, "Are you applying as a student or as a lecturer?" I smiled, as I had already noticed her expression when she looked at my CV. Then she decided to be cheeky and added, "Wow, you're forty-five, I will be forty-four in a few months!"

Yes, I am, duh! Thanks for letting me know we're mates. I am not the first mature student and I will not be the last. 'Scuse me, mate, let me be!

What a cheeky somebody! LOL

When I completed the Access course, I began to make applications to universities. At some point, I thought, *"Funmi, why don't you just continue your job as a healthcare assistant?* (By this time, I had started a job as a healthcare assistant). *Do you really want to put yourself through another three years of studying?"*

I began to think I was going through a midlife crisis (MLC). In fact, when a friend of mine who I told that I was going back to university reminded me that I would be nearly fifty years by the time I graduated, I began to conclude in my mind that this indeed must be MLC. But on second thought, my attitude was, *"What do I care? Since life has decided to throw me this lemon. I am prepared to make a lemonade out of it."*

All I knew was that there was more to me than settling for what any situation had thrown at me.

Off to university, I went, and proudly too. I got admission into all my five choices but chose the campus that I would not have to travel too far to. I wanted, just as with college, a situation where I would be leaving home and getting back about the same time as my two girls. That was important to me.

As should be expected, university was hard work - especially considering my age - but it was also fun. (Well, I decided to make it so!) I did not just pass through the university, but I let the university pass through me. Trust me, even though I was on a Nursing course, I went for any free business training organised by the Student Enterprise of the university. Every opportunity available to learn something new, I jumped at. We were not very many in my cohort, but we were a "crazy" bunch. I guess we needed people with a great sense of humour because of the nature of the clients that we would be working with. Life is hard enough. We studied hard and we played hard. At some point during the course, we went on a one-week trip to Germany for a conference.

In my third year, I was voted as the class representative. Many of my younger classmates who were of African descent and knew that I was not a youth (LOL) called me "Aunty", while some called me "Sis." But then, who said I was not a youth - when the Bible tells me that my youth is renewed like the eagle's (Psalm 103:5)? In fact, borrowing their words, I was living my best life!

Find Melodies, Make Memories

One of the many interesting experiences I had was while on my first placement at university. It was at a school for people with special needs. My special little people.... oh, you've got to love them! It was time for recess and all the children were out in the playground, having fun. Except for this cute little boy who decided he did not want to play outside but stay in the classroom and play with some toys. (We would often **offer** them a choice). One of the teaching assistants (TA), and I stayed with him. The teaching assistant then excused herself to go to the bathroom, and I was alone with "Mister Cute".

I sat on the chair and he was on the floor beside me playing with some of his favourite toys, or so I thought. A few minutes later, I turned to pick up something from the floor, and the next thing I saw was something flying right before my eyes across the room. I realised that this looked like a chunk of hair. I thought for a moment that it was a doll's hair, until I realised it was my hair! I mean, my wig! *No, it cannot be!* I had to touch my head to confirm I was not imagining things. My little friend had decided to remove my wig, as in, at lightning speed, and thrown it across the room. He then went back to continue what he was doing, like nothing had happened.

My first expression was shock. I was so shocked at how fast he did that and wondered how he knew I had a wig on. I wasn't sure he could not have tried to take out my head! By this time, the other TA had come back, and when she saw what had happened, we both burst into laughter. We even had to call the other TAs to come and see what had just happened. Interestingly, they hadn't even known it was a wig I had on – it was a short natural-looking wig. Thank God, I had a wig cap on. We all had a good laugh.

When something unexpected happens in our lives, we are forced to make a decision, and whatever decision we make can either make us or break us. We do not grow when things are easy; we grow when we face challenges. Growth comes when we respond to adversity by stretching just an edge beyond our talent and experience. Take the best out of everything and adapt it to your needs. Take stock of all you have been through.

Where there is no adversity, there is no growth. Adversity is one of the most powerful forces in life that can either bring out the worst in you or make you a much better person. At the end of the day, it is up to you. I have seen the approach to adversity play out in the lives of many individuals but unfortunately the most common response to adversity is to try and make it go away. The reality is that when you take away adversity, you also take away one of the most important ingredients to greatness.

Reflect and Resolve

So, let me ask: Will you allow the obstacles surrounding you to be roadblocks or springboards? Will that adversity turn your focus from getting better to getting bitter? Or will you see adversity-laced setbacks as true gifts and growth accelerators that can provide you the opportunity to believe in yourself, revitalise your commitment to what you intend to achieve, and also reassess what you are willing to sacrifice to make it happen?

They say what does not kill you makes you stronger. The hardships and misfortunes you've been through can give you the confidence that you are capable of handling whatever comes your way. You have been in tough times before; how did you emerge victorious? What got you through? Your past experiences can help you find your inner strength and resilience.

Author Maya Angelou once said during an interview, "We may encounter many defeats, but we must not be defeated. It may even be necessary to encounter the defeat, so that we can know who we are. So that we can see, oh, that happened, and I rose. I did get knocked down flat in front of the whole world, and I rose. I did not run away -- I rose right where I'd been knocked down. And then that's how you get to know yourself."

That is the spirit you should adopt.

As Haruki Murakami rightly said, *"And once the storm is over, you won't remember how you made it through, how you managed to survive. You won't even be sure, whether the storm is really over. But one thing is certain. When you come out of the storm, you won't be the same person who walked in. That's what this storm's all about."*

CHAPTER 4

THINK LIKE A CHAMPION

"While we may not be able to control all that happens to us, we can control what happens inside us."

- Benjamin Franklin

Sometimes, the challenge we have in dealing with adversity is that we worry too much. *What if I go through all the work to make a change, and it does not work out? Or even worse, what if it is not what I want after all?*

Edwin Locke, one of the foremost researchers in goal setting, states that the number one thing that stands in the way of goal attainment is fear. Fear of failure, fear of success, fear of the unknown, fear of making the wrong decision, fear of looking foolish, fear of being embarrassed and so on.

Combine the fear of taking a risk with a lack of energy to work toward our goals, and a lack of confidence in our abilities, and it's no wonder we stay locked in our old habits and routines despite our unhappiness.

But, really, why bother striving for new opportunities, or working to change a current situation that is not optimal? What do we really have to gain?

Carolyn Adams-Miller, author of Creating Your Best Life List, says that when we engage in a well-planned risk, even if it is scary, we immediately gain confidence, make progress toward goal accomplishment and enjoy an increase in our life satisfaction. Even when the risk does not turn out exactly as hoped, we still benefit. We learn that we can handle whatever curveballs life throws at us and increase our resilience (the ability to bounce back after disappointment).

Together, these experiences increase our inner strength and lead us to be more willing to try new and different experiences in the future. And isn't that what makes life exciting?

Building Blocks of Positivity

The following principles will help you to develop a positive mindset in adversity.

- **Use the power of imagination**

This is the ability to envision in your mind what you cannot at present see with your eyes. It is based on the principle that all things are created twice, first in the mental and then in the physical. The physical creation follows the mental, just as a building follows a blueprint. Before I set out to start writing this book, I had a blueprint. I created an idea mind map and a how-to mind map that helped me to structure my writing. And I had a mental picture of what I wanted the book to look like once it is published. And off to work I went.

You cannot bring to life what you have not imagined in your mind. If you are a Christian, you can easily translate this to mean that the spiritual also controls the physical. With this understanding, you can visualise, through the eyes of the spirit, who you are meant to be in life and the kind of life you're supposed to be living. Fortunately for you, there are manifold promises and declarations in the Scripture that describe who you are as a child of God. The onus then is on you to begin to see yourself as God sees you. When you see Scripture verses like the ones below, what do you think of yourself?

Psalms 139:14 - "I will praise you, for I am fearfully and wonderfully made".

Jeremiah 29:11 – For I know the thoughts that I think toward you, says the Lord, thoughts of peace and not of evil, to give you a future and a hope".

Philippians 4:13 – "I can do all things through Christ who strengthens me".

Mathew 11:28 – "Come to me, all you who labour and are heavy laden, and I will give you rest."

If you do not make a conscious effort to visualise who you are and what you want in life, then you empower other people and circumstances to shape you and your life by default. It is about connecting again with your own uniqueness and then defining the spiritual, personal, and ethical guidelines within which you can most happily express and fulfil yourself.

One of the best ways to incorporate the power of imagination into your life is to develop a Personal Mission Statement. It focuses on what you want to be and do. It is your plan for success. It reaffirms who you are, puts your goals in focus, and moves your ideas into the real world. Your mission statement makes you the leader of your own life. You create your own destiny and secure the future you envision.

- **Be mentally prepared**

"I am prepared for the worst but hope for the best." More than 185 years after these words were written by British Prime Minister, Benjamin Disraeli, they still inspire. Being prepared means thinking through the worst-case scenarios and considering how you would respond.

What would your plan of action be if adversity happens? Running through potential disasters on a regular basis builds mental strength and flexibility to overcome mishaps or catastrophes in real life. It does not mean you should dwell on negative possibilities. But if the worst happens, having thought through how you would react will keep you from panicking and help you stay rational. It will not feel so frightening because you will not be caught completely off guard.

If you think about it, every choice we make in life holds some degree of risk. Each time we get into a car, fly in a plane, or cross the street, we are taking risks. When you approach that person who caught your eye, you risk being rejected, but might also meet the love of your life. If you choose an out-of-the-ordinary restaurant, you might not enjoy your meal; or then again, it could be the best you've ever tasted.

Although these examples are minor risks, as compared to choices that can lead to life-changing events, Todd Kashdan, Ph.D., author of the book, Curious, believes that most people overestimate risk, failure and danger, while underestimating the value of being curious. He writes, "We can, and should, choose how we want to live our lives. Are we governed by fear and the need for safety, or are we willing to accept a bit of risk and anxiety in the pursuit of satisfaction, growth and meaning?"

- **Keep a positive mindset**

A healthy dose of optimism goes a long way when you are faced with a bad situation. It may seem cliché, but sometimes the darkest storm clouds really do have silver linings. It turns out that developing a positive mindset is an important coping skill when dealing with adversity.

It is true you need to be realistic and see a situation clearly, but if you constantly frame everything in a negative way, you will only see the bad. Try cultivating positivity and refuse to let pessimistic voices and naysayers invade your mind.

 Enjoy where you are on the way to where you are going. Do not stop living.

That was exactly what I did on my journey to starting again. I never stopped living. Even though I was not where I knew I should be then, I decided to take on this adventure in full stride. I took every phase as an opportunity to learn new things. I knew who I was and understood that this could only be but a phase. With every difficulty that came with each phase, I knew I had to finish this race, otherwise I would not reach my desired destination.

For the change we desire in our next season to happen, we need to begin to develop the power of an extraordinary mind. It is time for a paradigm shift - an elevated mind, a re-alignment of our thoughts, a shift back to our original nature. Begin to go back to what the promises of God are for your life. You need to upgrade your thoughts to upgrade your life; you cannot give room to stagnancy. When you change, everyone around you will notice and not only will they accommodate your change, but you will also begin to influence them to greater things too.

- **Live by faith**

The provisions and resources that we need to live in life generally are by-products of our faith. We finish our education, and we have faith that we will get into employment or start a business. All the things we do to accomplish those phases in our lives, we do by faith. It is no different when we find ourselves going through adversity. We need to continue to live by faith. God will not give us more than we can bear (1 Corinthians 10:13). The situation may be difficult and unpleasant at the time, but we are rest assured that He will never leave or forsake us. He will guide and direct us to people and places where we will find help for that journey, if only we can just trust the process. I remember times in my journey when I could not afford the basic things I needed, but my faith began to grow as I exercised it daily.

- **Reject negative influences**

It is impossible to completely remove all the "noise" from your life, but you can choose how you filter, process, and respond to it—and it is extremely important that you do so, because your subconscious processes these emotions, regardless of whether you are actively or passively allowing them to penetrate your psyche. The negative emotions to be particularly wary of include fear, worry, and self-doubt, as these emotions colour our dominating thoughts in such a way as to diminish our agency and faith in our ability to persevere and succeed; instead, we open ourselves up to being consumed by helplessness, which manifests either in inaction or frenzy.

To reduce your vulnerability to negative influences and emotions, cultivate an awareness that negative influences harmonise the most with your weaknesses, as these are the ones to which you will be the most susceptible. In addition, assess your inner circle to ensure it consists only of supportive individuals who will encourage you to think and act for yourself. For those negative individuals in your personal and professional spheres with whom you must regularly interact, establish firm boundaries about the information they share in your presence.

- **Harness the power of decision**

Because negative emotions and influences tend to work us into a state of inaction, the greatest antidote to them is decisiveness. Making firm decisions enables us to create momentum in a constructive direction. A similar principle to the one behind exposure therapy is at play here: If we consistently decide to act toward our dreams, despite our negative emotions, then we can disempower them by incrementally confronting them.

Self-discipline and willpower are crucial here. We must keep our definite chief aim at the forefront of our mind and not allow negative influences, whether external or internal, to throw us off course.

Bottom-line

It is important to get yourself into a resourceful and positive place to forge ahead during adversity. It is through our struggles in adversity or crisis that we can learn some of life's most important lessons. Having the ability therefore to face adversity head-on will allow you to build resilience that will not only help you overcome your situation but will also prepare you to better handle future challenges. And sometimes setbacks are an opportunity for us to change our plans and reinvent ourselves.

The ability to not only embrace adversity, but also find opportunities to better a situation is what separates the successful from the underachiever. Your mind is a powerful thing. When you fill it with positive thoughts, your life will start to change.

Once your mindset changes, everything on the outside will change along with it.

CHAPTER 5

THE WINNING ATTITUDE

"It is your attitude more than your aptitude that will determine your altitude".

- Zig Ziglar

I wholeheartedly buy into the above quote by Ziglar. Research has shown that attitude is a better predictor of success than IQ, grade point average or almost any other factor you can think of. Dr Martin Seligman proved this in his ground-breaking book, *Learned Optimism.* He found that negative people get sick more often, are divorced more frequently, and raise kids who get in more trouble.

Seligman even found that negative people make less money. In one long-term study of 1500 people, group A or 83 per cent of the people took their jobs because they believed they could make lots of money. Only 17 per cent of them — or group B — took their jobs because they happened to love their jobs. Twenty years later, the two groups had produced 101 millionaires. The amazing thing is, only one of those millionaires came from group A; the remaining 100 of them came from group B. That is significant.

Even more amazing is that over 70 per cent of those millionaires never went to college. And over 70 per cent of those who became CEOs graduated in the bottom half of their class. Seligman concluded that it was their attitude, more than their aptitude, which determined their altitude. Wow!

You Hold the Key

It's a ridiculously huge misconception to say, "I can't help the way I feel. That's just the way I am". The truth is you can help the way you feel, and you can change the way you are. You may not know how, or find it difficult to, but your attitude is totally changeable and controllable. You cannot always choose what happens to you, but you can always choose what happens in you. You cannot always control what someone does to you, but you can always control how you respond to what they do to you.

These are statements that I have chosen to live by and that has helped me tremendously in every area of my life. Sometimes people think nothing bothers you when you choose to live this way. The fact is, some things in life are beyond our control, while some others are within it. So, my attitude in these areas - whether beyond my control or within my control - will make the difference in the outcome that I get out of the situation or circumstance.

This is why your attitude can either be an asset or a liability. Your attitude can lift you up or bring you down. It is what makes or breaks you. When you have a positive mental attitude, you might not be able to do everything, but it will help you do anything better than you would if your attitude were negative.

A positive attitude is a game changer amid adversity. History has it that Abraham Lincoln - American statesman who served as the 16th president of the United States of America - despite repeated losses in various elections, a difficult marriage, the nation falling apart, one thing stood out, and that was that he lived and led with an indomitable positive attitude. This was a choice he made. No wonder, he once said: "Most people are about as happy as they make up their minds to be".

It is possible to lose your self-esteem, reach a point of frustration or even a stage of depression when you can no longer do the things you were once able to do. There is no denying the fact that this can destabilise and destroy your morale, but a positive attitude will help provide a positive framework from which you can approach the issue and guide your steps to reaching a possible solution.

Bounce Back Strategy

Getting back into paid employment was taking longer than I expected. As I revealed earlier, I had stopped "signing on" by now, but I knew I needed to look for something to do. I needed to earn again. At some point, while applying for jobs, a particularly good friend of mine said she was looking for someone to pick up her children after school and keep them till when she came back from work. Yes, so I offered myself as her child-minder for a few months, and I even took on another child at the time.

After that season passed, I went on to work as a domiciliary carer. I did not like the fact that I had to drive - sometimes to long distances - only to do a half-hour job, possibly twice a day. So, a younger friend reluctantly suggested I apply for a permanent healthcare assistant (HCA) role in a care home. I say "reluctant" because she wasn't sure how well I would take the offer as she knew I was a professional who had worked in the city for a long period of time, and working as an HCA meant taking up a role beneath my qualifications. At that point, all I wanted to do was anything that would bring in £££, and anyway, I yearned to experience something new.

So, I applied for this role, got the job, and ignorantly asked to do a 48-hour shift. That should be a walk in the park, right? After all, I was used to working long hours sometimes as an accountant, especially when we had to balance the books. Oh boy, was I in for a rude shock! A 12-hour shift, four days a week, and after just one month, I was like, "I am a celebrity, get me out of here!" What?? It is not a job for the fainthearted at all. The long hours of standing, the backache, phew! But I loved to look after the residents, I enjoyed the interaction and getting them to participate in activities.

I reached out to the manager of the care home and explained my dilemma to her. She laughed at me, knowing that I had originally wanted to start with a 60-hour shift, and she had advised me to start on a 48-hour shift. Also, she knew that I was new to the health care sector and would need a bit of time to adjust. Anyway, she suggested that I opt to work as a bank staff, which meant that I got to choose the hours I worked when shifts became available. I thought that was a good idea and afforded me some flexibility, so I could still get to pursue other interests. I started to do the bank shifts. It still was not easy, but I knew it was just a phase and this too shall pass. I would take my iPad with me and during my breaks would surf the net, read articles, and do a lot of research on subjects of interest.

Thing is, when you come from a totally different career background into the healthcare profession (or any other profession at that), you must be prepared for a change in mindset. I am very organised and meticulous by nature, and I like to do things by the book (the accountant in me). This can sometimes cause friction and opposition when you find yourself working in a place that does not adopt a similar culture. But one thing I did was I maintained a positive attitude - a winning attitude. I knew that for me to survive my time there, I had to adapt to the ways of working, without compromising my values. And that was what I did, and this made me to find favour with my colleagues and the managers. Because they knew my professional background, I immediately became a favourite candidate for planning and drawing up the monthly shifts on a spreadsheet.

Model of Positive Attitude

A winning attitude will help you to enjoy where you are on the way to where you are going.

I once read an article, titled "The Toll Booth Experience", by Dr Charles Garfield, detailing a model of a positive attitude. I am sure you will find this as inspiring as I did. Dr Garfield writes:

"If you have ever gone through a toll booth, you know that your relationship with the person in the booth is not the most intimate you'll ever have. It is one of life's frequent non-encounters. You hand over some money - you might get change - you drive off. I have been through every one of the 17 toll booths on the Oakland-San Francisco Bay Bridge on thousands of occasions and never had an exchange worth remembering with anybody.

Late one morning in 1984, headed for lunch in San Francisco, I drove toward one of the booths. I heard loud music. It sounded like a party, or a Michael Jackson concert. I looked around. No other cars with their windows open. No sound trucks. I looked at the toll booth. Inside it, the man was dancing.

"What are you doing?" I asked. "I'm having a party," he said. "What about the rest of the people?" I looked over at other booths; nothing moving there. "They're not invited."

I had a dozen other questions for him, but somebody in a big hurry to get somewhere started punching his horn behind me and I drove off. But I made a note to myself: Find this guy again. There is something in his eye that says there's magic in his toll booth.

Months later I did find him again, still with the loud music, still having a party. Again, I asked, "What are you doing?"

He said, "I remember you from the last time. I am still dancing. I'm having the same party." I said, "Look. What about the rest of the people?"

He said, "Stop. What do those look like to you?" He pointed down the row of toll booths. "They look like...toll booths," I replied. "Nooooo imagination!" I said, "Okay, I give up. What do they look like to you?" He said, "Vertical coffins."

"What are you talking about?" "I can prove it. At 8:30 every morning, living people get in. Then they die for eight hours. At 4:30, like Lazarus from the dead, they re-emerge and go home. For eight hours, their brain is on hold, dead on the job. Going through the motions."

I was amazed. This guy had developed a philosophy, a mythology about his job. I could not help asking the next question: "Why is it different for you? You're having a good time."

He looked up at me. "I knew you were going to ask that," he said. "I'm going to be a dancer someday." He pointed to the administration building. "My bosses are in there and they're paying for my training."

Sixteen people dead on the job, and the seventeenth, in precisely the same situation, figured out a way to live. That man was having a party where you and I would probably not last three days. The boredom! He and I did have lunch later, and he said, "I don't understand why anybody would think my job is boring. I have a corner office, glass on all sides. I can see the Golden Gate, San Francisco, the Berkeley hills; half the Western world vacations here...and I just stroll in every day and practice dancing."

I fell in love with this narrative when I first read it. It just shows that the circumstance you find yourself in does not have to define you; you can choose to define the circumstance. What do you think separates the best people from the rest? What do you think makes it possible for one person to thrive after going through an adversity while another person gives up? It is their attitude.

Choose the Brighter Side

Attitude is a criterion for success, but it is not what you can buy. Everybody can have a good attitude when things are going well. But what happens when situations in your life become unpleasant? Do not allow adversity to have an adverse effect on your attitude.

A person's attitude is not set; it is a choice. We have a choice each day regarding the attitude we embrace for that day. We may not be able to change the past, we may not be able to change the fact that people act in certain ways, we may not be able to change the inevitable, but one thing we certainly have control over is our attitude. Pastor Chuck Swindoll says it well, *"I am convinced that life is 10 percent what happens to me and 90 percent how I react to it."*

CHAPTER 6

GOLDMINES OF ADVERSITY

"Opportunity is missed by most people because it is dressed in overalls and looks like work.

- Thomas Edison

The premise of the above quote by the renowned American inventor is simple - there is hardly a shortcut to success. Success is nearly always the result of work, sometimes a lot of work. But the bigger point of the quotation is that people often miss an opportunity when it is presented - because the work required makes the opportunity less appealing.

One of the biggest ironies of life is how often people complain about their circumstances, yet rarely do anything about them. It is not that they do not have good intentions or the desire for change. The problem is that change can appear scary because of the risks involved. So, even when we are unhappy with our current situation, we become too familiar with it. Change is just so unknown, thereby making us miss opportunities too often, even when they are staring us in the face. When we find ourselves going through adversities, we can become so embroiled in fear that we spend more time thinking about the situation rather than doing something about it.

Generally, most of us live by routines. A lot of times we travel through life on autopilot. We get up at a particular time, prepare for the day, and embark on the myriad of responsibilities we need to attend to. Sometimes we do not give much thought to these responsibilities, but we just go through the motions of getting things done, crossing them off our lists, and on we move to the next. We may then reach a stage where we begin to ask ourselves, "Is this all there is to me?" We begin to get restless and there is a yearning for a change. When we begin to feel this unrest within us, we know that it is time to look for new opportunities.

This is not different when we go through adversity, or when a change occurs in our lives; it may be time to start looking for new opportunities. At this point, we should start dreaming of what change we would like to see. Whether it is starting a new job, moving to a new house, finding love again, starting that business or writing that book, there are opportunities all around to help us fulfil these yearnings, if we dare to look.

Note, however, that success tends to be more likely when preparation precedes the opportunity. The two must work hand-in-hand but people sometimes want one without the other. You might question the need for preparation when you are not sure that the opportunity you desire will come, but I tell you, there is no wasted learning. You will soon find out that whatever preparation you devote yourself to will ultimately stand you in good stead when opportunity presents itself.

Maximise Each Opportunity

Be sensitive to opportunities in your journey and embrace them. Many people wait for conditions to be perfect. Do what you must do before you can do what you want to do. Be humble enough to do whatever is legitimate for you to put food on your table. Take whatever opportunity that comes your way, even if it is not your first choice. Volunteer or take on temporary posts. There is dignity in labour.

Quit feeling sorry for yourself, make a move. Sometimes a different road takes you to where you were meant to be. Never in my wildest imagination would I have thought that I would at some point in my life take on the role of a healthcare assistant. It was what needed to be done at the time, and I must say it opened doors of opportunities for me beyond my imagination.

At the time I decided to go back to college, I did not have to pay tuition fees as I was eligible for grants and bursaries for adult learners. Now, I did not know that was possible at the time, until I began to explore what was available. Once college was over and it was time to apply to university, I was one of the last sets of students that were eligible for help with tuition fees for Nursing before it was scrapped. I could have missed that opportunity if I had not made a move at the time I did.

In my second year at university, I was approached by the then mayor in the borough where I lived, to ask that I be one of her disability champions during her mayoral year. Wow, I was elated and, of course, I jumped at the opportunity. I must emphasise one point, however: that opportunity would not have arisen if I had not looked for opportunities to serve within my community while I was out of work, and also if I hadn't chosen the course I was studying. Volunteering is an opportunity that can open unimaginable doors to you. (I will discuss the place of service and volunteering in the next chapter).

Do the Incredible

We each face adversity in our individual ways, but the people who are ultimately successful in their endeavours are often those who find ways to create opportunities out of their adversity.

In his self-help classic, *Think and Grow Rich*, Napoleon Hill proclaims, "Never has there been a time more favourable to pioneers than the present." And yet, as at when Hill was writing those words, America was at the tail-end of the worst economic downturn in history. *Think and Grow Rich* was published in March 1937, right before the nation experienced a recession while still preoccupied with recovery efforts from the Great Depression. To put it in perspective: The unemployment rate in May 1937 was at 14.3 per cent and would continue an upward trajectory to reach 20 per cent in 1938. In comparison, the unemployment rate in April 2020 peaked at 14.7 per cent and by June had decreased to a still substantial 11.1 per cent.

Despite the bleak outlook in the 1930s, Hill was emphatic about the potential for incredible success for those who reframed their perspective on challenges and took consistent action towards achieving their definite chief aim. In fact, in *Think and Grow Rich*, he goes so far as to claim that "the 'depression' was a blessing in disguise" because it "reduced the whole world to a new starting point that gives everyone a new opportunity." In other words, it levelled the playing field, clearing the way for entrepreneurs who lacked the resources of the corporate giants to build their businesses.

Similarly, we can approach the "new normal" brought on by the current global pandemic as an opportunity for entrepreneurs, organisations, and society at large to regroup, reset, and create better pathways to success.

Can you see the new starting point that Hill referred to now? Do you see an opportunity in this "new normal"? There is no better time to begin to seek out opportunities in these unprecedented times, but you will need to reframe your perspective on adversity.

Obstacles and adversities often conceal the seeds of success. As Hill goes on to write, opportunity "has the sly habit of slipping in by the back door, and often it comes disguised in the form of misfortune, or temporary defeat." This is likely why, he notes, so many people miss out on life-changing opportunities.

Seek New Pathways

As difficult as it may seem, we need to shift our mindset so that we can identify the possibilities in pivoting the opportunities that challenges provide. This is not a naïve, "silver lining" mentality. It is okay—even necessary—to acknowledge the weight of our feelings about adversity, but we should use those emotions to drive us forward toward our dreams, rather than allowing them to keep us stuck grieving a lost path. Remember, there are many roads to success, and just because one happened to be our favourite does not mean that it was the right one for us. If we hold tightly to our expectations on how our plans should have gone, our focus will be too narrow to recognise the most valuable opportunities for originality, growth, and connection.

For instance, perhaps an unexpected job loss provides you with the chance to leverage your experience and expertise and build your own business as a freelancer. It truly takes an open, enlarged mindset to be able to see an obstacle from a new angle—a perspective that oftentimes will shift our perception of it.

There is no time better than this for us to begin to identify new opportunities for collaboration and innovation. Many businesses right now are flourishing because they have pivoted by building connections and collaborating across industries. How can you expand your network to include diverse perspectives that complement and enrich your own? By creating new partnerships, particularly those focused on adding value to the lives of others, we can find new ways to serve our customers and clients while creating new pathways for prosperity for ourselves and the larger world. The pandemic has revealed the ways in which we are dynamically interconnected.

As Hill encourages us in his 1952 speech, "Maker of Miracle Men": "If there was ever a time in this country when men and women need to recognise the power of their own minds...that time is now.... Let us get our minds, each one of us as individuals, fixed upon a definite goal so big and so outstanding that we'll have no time to think about these things we don't want."

What this means is that by reframing our perspective on adversity, we can use the current climate, difficult as it is, as an opportunity for creativity and a springboard for success.

No Risk, No Wreath

Life is about taking risks. If you refuse to take risks, you are depriving yourself of so many chances you can maximise if you try. In order to seize an opportunity, you must be willing to take a risk. To grow, you must be willing to make mistakes. To reach your potential, you must be willing to take chances. Failure to do any of these means choosing to resign to a life of mediocrity.

A famous quote of Ayn Rand's is, "The ladder of success is best climbed by stepping on the rungs of opportunity."

And many - I am not sure who first did - have said, "When looking back over my life, I don't regret the things I did, just the things I never did."

Are you ready to embrace the mindset of an optimist, climb the ladder of success and eliminate future regrets? Then seize your next opportunity, and see what doors open for you! Make an incredible pivot during unprecedented times. It is your reality!

"A pessimist sees the difficulty in every opportunity; an optimist sees the opportunity in every difficulty." So said Winston Churchill.

CHAPTER 7

MAKING THE RIGHT MOVES

"You don't have to be great to start, but you have to start to be great."

- Joe Sabah

It is human nature to have a constant desire for growing, evolving, and changing. If you are stuck in a routine for too long, you are likely to get a feeling of boredom, a desire for change - or the despair that comes from the feelings of underachievement. Sometimes, however, it is adversity that forces us to change.

Whatever the case may be for you, it is always good practice to sit back, reflect, and gain clarity about your current circumstances, and where you will desire to be, going forward. Most of the time, this is where we get stuck. We know we need a change; we know we need to overcome this difficult situation somehow, but we are not clear as to how to go about it. We must be intentional about taking the steps required to take us to that desired state.

It is time to start moving forward. After all, you cannot expect to overcome a challenging situation in your life if you do not make a move. You now need to begin to put things into perspective. It is the perfect time to come up with an escape plan from your current situation. When you see the vision of where you want to be, you can start to fill in the details with a direction to start moving in. The key here is to make the decision to move forward consciously and intentionally and have a solid action plan to follow.

Here is what to do:

1. Take one step at a time.

You need to be mindful that whatever changes you need to make will begin with taking one step at a time. There is a tendency - especially if you have been there, done that - to want to speed things up to get you back up to the status quo. You may feel that the odds are stacked against you in life, and you are having to start from the beginning. So, what?

Every person who has ever achieved something significant has had to overcome the odds. Remember that you are now possibly exploring new territories, and you will need time to manoeuvre and adapt to this new space. Moreover, you are not in competition with anyone; your focus should be to get back up on your feet and do it more powerfully.

I have often said that the person who is having to start all over due to adversity is not now starting from scratch but starting from experience. You have prior experience to your advantage, which you can put to good use, and it must be visible in this new journey. For you, it is now not about finding yourself, it is about establishing yourself.

Make humility your watchword Seriously, I have seen many people miss it big time because of pride. As the saying goes, "Pride goes before a fall." I am not saying that all adversities are because of pride, but there cannot be a rising without humility. It is possible that God wants to take you through a journey of learning or discovery, and he can choose whichever way He wants to do that so that His name can ultimately be glorified. Humility is strength, not weakness. Humility is a great strength. In the beatitudes, Jesus teaches us, "Blessed are the meek, for they shall inherit the earth" (Matthew 5:5). The meek are not weak. The meek understand the power of finding our sufficiency in Christ, and they rest in it. The assurance we have from the Lord Himself is, "My grace is sufficient for you, for My strength is made perfect in weakness" (2 Corinthians 12:9). We can truly live a humble life only when we are secure in our calling and our identity in Christ. We must acknowledge the work of Christ in our lives and our dependence upon Him. Humility is best demonstrated when I know my rights and my position so well that I do not even have to contend or defend. I am not insecure in who I am or in my mission. I am not easily frustrated when challenged, because I know who I am and what I am about. A posture of humility is a posture of quiet strength.

I remembered having to swallow my "pride" after I was made redundant, and now had to take on all sorts of "unprofessional roles". I did not take up any of those roles with an attitude of, "Hey, you better respect me because I was once a professional. I worked in the city of London and I was on such and such salary." Believe me, most times when I got paid for those roles, I remembered my salary as an accountant, and it hurt. But that did not stop me from giving my best on the job. It was now not about the role I was handling; it was about the value I was bringing to the role. That was the key that made me stand out and positioned me back to where I originally was meant to be. I was not sure why redundancy happened to me. I was not sure why I did not get another job at the time with the same or equivalent salary; but I knew that there was a shift, which might not be clear to me then, but which would surely be revealed to me as I maintained a humble posture. After all, if I could make things happen in my power or strength, I would not be in the situation that I found myself in.

Giving a clear picture of what humility entails, Fela Durotoye, leadership coach and transformational speaker, said: "Humility is the acknowledgement of the nothingness that you are, but for the grace of God. Humility therefore is the container of grace. And it is that grace that works on your effort to give supernatural effect – this is what makes you produce results. As humility is to grace, so is the absence of humility to dis-grace. When you think that you are better than others, or when you exhibit arrogance of knowledge, that is, thinking your expertise/experience makes you better than someone else, humiliation is inevitable. Humiliation will therefore make you come to the point where you will need grace."

Those were some of the many words I heard during the Speak for Gold Masterclass facilitated by Durotoye, and I was just so wowed by those words. Sitting in a virtual class with this one-time presidential aspirant of the Federal Republic of Nigeria, and hearing those words come out of him, I knew that this man was an epitome of humility - a true leader in every form. And this was evident in his interactions with everyone who was in the class.

Another great example of a great leader and humility personified is Pastor Gbolahan Bright (MBE) who has kindly written a foreword for this book. Pastor Bright was there during my college days when I would sit most evenings in the local library and study for my exams. Though much older than I was, he would accord me so much respect, encourage me and pray with me. In fact, one of the major events that I anchored was one organised by him - the celebration of Her Majesty, the Queen of England's 90th birthday anniversary in 2016, in our borough. I was elated when he came to the library and said to me, "Ma, we have a big event coming up and I would like you to be the Mistress of Ceremonies (MC)."

Remember, purpose was still finding me while I was doing what I needed to do. Pastor Gbolahan Bright was awarded an MBE because of his services in helping students succeed in their academics by offering free Mathematics tutorials then. Despite this achievement, he remained ever humble.

The Scripture confirms that pride goes before a fall. 1 Peter 5:5-6 says, "God resists the proud, but gives grace to the humble. Therefore, humble yourselves under the mighty hand of God, that He may exalt you in due time."

Your due time is coming if you will choose to walk in humility.

Humility is determined by the way we see ourselves. If we see ourselves as superior, we will treat others according to our mindset. If we see ourselves as nothing, we will debase and demean ourselves out of our emotional instability, and unfortunately, we will demean others, because that is how we see ourselves. This means that humility is neither a superior attitude, nor is its self-demeaning; rather, it is an attitude that finds joy in the joy and transformation of others. Humility will make you stand out even amid adversity. Baptist preacher, John Bunyan, said it very beautifully, "He that is down needs fear no fall. He that is low no pride. He that is humble ever shall have God to be his guide."

2. Be open to learning new things

Learning new things brings inspiration, and inspiration brings hope, desire, and positivity. We know we live in a world that is constantly changing. We therefore need to work to evolve ourselves, as this is critical to our success. Even when we know the purpose for which we were created, our assignment within our purpose continually evolves.

There are so many opportunities around us to learn new skills. The Internet world, in particular, is your oyster; there are so many free courses to choose from. And if you must pay to upgrade your skills, then please do. Ironically, I have found that it can sometimes be easier for us to spend on irrelevant things than it is to invest in ourselves. It is a choice you must make. I learnt many new skills during my period of waiting to get back into employment. You can also look for and attend relevant seminars and conferences.

3. Volunteer for service

The benefits of volunteering are huge. Helping in my local community was a big advantage in exposing me to a wealth of knowledge. It opened opportunities to plan and coordinate medium-scale events and exhibitions, as well as to build my network. These are things I had a passion for anyway, so that proved to be another platform to showcase and expand my skills and knowledge. I had also always volunteered in various capacities in my local church. And oh, can I say that I came away with numerous recognitions and awards as a result!

Evidence has shown that people who volunteer have higher self-esteem and overall well-being. Experts explain that as feelings of social connectedness increase, so does your self-esteem. You cannot afford to isolate yourself when you are going through adversity. Volunteering is a way to develop your confidence, and the more regularly you volunteer, the greater your confidence becomes.

Volunteering is also a way of giving back. It makes you feel a sense of belonging and can help reduce loneliness and isolation. Helping others gives you a fresh perspective on your own situation and teaches you to be appreciative of what you have. Moreover, participating in volunteering work will leave you feeling fulfilled and empowered. If you really want to overcome your situation - not just endure but make it an adventure - you need to start changing your status quo. Discover and pursue a life that brings progress and positive changes to your world. Surround yourself with people who care about you, want the best for you, and believe in you.

The most important factor, however, is to remember that you are not alone. Sometimes, it may seem easier to just cope, endure and put on a happy face, but it is not. Trust me, it is more difficult to remain a victim of your circumstance.

4. Serve someone else's vision

Never be too big to help someone else fulfil their own vision. This is an excellent way to learn humility. Great leaders are great followers. By serving someone else's vision, you make someone look great rather than yourself. You are also learning to lead and gaining lots of experience in the process. You learn the secrets of managing people and time, dealing with pressure, and much more. If you are blessed to serve under a good leader, you are open to lots of support, encouragement, and mentoring. The true change happens when you fully embrace the relationships and connections around you.

You need to be intentional about taking the appropriate steps to prepare for your next season. But remember, good intentions never produce any results if they are not backed up by action.

Intentional living means making choices for your life, based on your values, not the habits of others.

CHAPTER 8

THE PILLAR OF ACCOUNTABILITY

"Ninety-nine percent of all failures come from people who have a habit of making excuses."

- George Washington Carver

Accountability issues have been around since Adam and Eve ate the apple in the Garden of Eden. Adam blamed Eve; Eve blamed the snake. Blaming others rarely works as a long-term solution. The snake's reward for its behaviour was a lifetime of crawling. Eve's reward was painful childbirth. Adam's reward was a lifetime of toil. Ha, thank God for Jesus!

My use of the word "reward" is deliberate. This is because accountability is a choice. The decisions we choose to make reward us with an outcome.

The first man and woman each made a choice to test the limits of the trust they had been given. They were told, "Of every tree of the garden you may freely eat; but of the tree of the knowledge of good and evil you shall not eat..." (Genesis 2:16-17). Despite this covenant or contract, Adam and Eve decided to eat the forbidden fruit, and their individual choices set off a chain of events for which they were rewarded.

Some may view the reward as "punishment." Others may see the result as the logical outcome of a poor choice made despite a clear set of expectations. Whatever your view, we have been struggling with accountability ever since.

You may have heard of the popular quote, "There are two primary choices in life: to accept conditions as they exist or accept the responsibility for changing them". These are the only two options we have; there is no in-between.

Take Responsibility

Most times, one of the things that we fail to do is to make ourselves accountable for the change we desire to happen. We expect someone else to make that change for us. Many who start on the journey of making the change struggle along the way or lose sight of their goals because they are not accountable to anyone.

The point here is that you must take responsibility for your life and be accountable for the things you do or say, regardless of circumstances. Learn to take responsibility for your seasons of change. This is not to say that you are responsible for causing the change, but that in acknowledging the season, you are accountable for how you react to it. You must actively take responsibility to respond properly to the change with the intent of participating in it and benefitting from it.

For example, you have a responsibility during this pandemic, to follow all guidelines that have been set to help prevent or transmit the COVID-19 virus. In abiding by these guidelines, you are playing your part in protecting yourself from being infected and preventing others from transmitting the infection. Having a responsible attitude towards this season therefore means that you understand your obligation to protect yourself, serve humanity, and do your part supporting God's good purposes for the earth.

Mirror of Introspection

Adversity is a great teacher. It can offer you the opportunity to gain valuable insights; to truly learn from your mistakes so you will have a better chance of success next time. However, you will have to engage in some self-reflection or introspection.

If you have failed in an endeavour, for instance, it may be necessary to engage in some self-examination and consider where and how things went wrong. It is time to take a careful look at your planning and preparation. Look at your execution. Did you put in consistent effort? As you think about the future, are you now beginning to take these things into consideration? Are you planning for any challenges that you may encounter ahead? Focus on the areas that are within your control and ask what more you can do next time.

When you are accountable for your response to a situation, you will not be moping around, feeling sorry for yourself or blaming others for what happened to you. Doing that can sabotage your ability to come up with solutions and the next steps forward.

It is important that you consider what mistakes or missteps you might have made. Spend time processing what you could have done differently and take responsibility for your actions. Make peace with what happened. Accept the situation for what it is, and then move on. As Steve Jobs said, "Sometimes when you innovate, you make mistakes. It's best to admit them quickly and get on with improving your other innovations."

Say No Evil, Hear No Evil

In times of adversity, you must be careful what you say. It is tempting to utter negative statements or lash out when we are under pressure, but we must realise that our words have consequences. At such times, be slow to speak and quick to hear. When you make negative pronouncements, you invoke negativity around you, which may ultimately begin to affect your thought process and put off those around you.

Make positive confessions and declarations into your life always.

Ephesians 4:29 counsels, "Let no corrupt word proceed out of your mouth, but what is good for necessary edification, that it may impart grace unto the hearers."

Be careful what you hear. Take heed of who or what you listen to. Surround yourself with people who will challenge you towards better thing; people who will encourage and pray with you. Listen to testimonies of people who have been through what you are going through and be encouraged by their words. Read books that expand your knowledge. Listen to music that edifies your soul. Remember, your faith is renewed by what you hear. Romans 10:17 says, "So then faith comes by hearing, and hearing by the word of God."

Be careful also of what you remember. Some people never let go of the past. They dwell so much on their past failures that they remain stuck in the rut of regret and indecision.

Negative memories have the power to influence our actions. Dwelling on past failures in your life can drag you down and make you a victim of your circumstance.

It is your responsibility to forgive and let go of anyone who has hurt you in one way or another. Release them in prayers so you can be free to all that God wants you to be. Holding on to what a person did to you is doing more damage to you than it can ever do to the person who hurt you.

God admonishes us not to be fixated on the past thus: "Do not remember the former things, nor consider the things of old. Behold, I will do a new thing, now it shall spring forth; shall you not know it? I will even make a road in the wilderness and rivers in the desert" (Isaiah 43:18-19).

The Accountability Partner

"As iron sharpens iron, so one man sharpens [and influences] another [through discussion]" (Proverbs 27:17, AMP)

One major problem that many people have is not having someone or group of persons to whom they are accountable. Having an accountability partner helps you to keep a commitment to a goal. It helps you to stay true to your course and accept responsibility for your goals.

Being accountable to someone helps to eliminate the time and effort you spend on distracting and unproductive activities. When you tell one or two trusted people about a project you want to embark on, or a goal you want to achieve, it helps to keep you on your toes, especially when they keep a track on your progress. Whenever you see them, you know you just must keep going. They are there to assist you along your journey.

An accountability partner may be your spouse, friend, colleague, mentor, coach, or family member, but you must be careful with your choice. You cannot just make anybody your accountability partner. In other words, in choosing an accountability partner, certain characteristics must be taken into consideration. Here are few tips to consider:

- Find someone who has a track record of success in the area you are venturing into. It is easier to learn from the experience of someone who has treaded the path you are planning to tread. They can hold you by the hand and guide you through that journey. They know what it takes, the hurdles to scale and the sacrifices to make to attain the goal.

- Choose someone that you look up to and will not want to disappoint. There are certain people in our lives that we would hate to disappoint. Who is that person who you cannot bear to let down, even if you may be willing to let yourself down? It may be because of the sacrifice they have made for you, or the fact that you know their success depends on yours. This may be a parent/carer or a child.

- Choose someone who is more disciplined than you. You cannot afford to have an undisciplined person as your accountability partner. If they do not bother about their own goals, why should they bother about yours? Someone who is disciplined and focused and does not take it easy on themselves will more than likely not take it easy on you.

- Choose a partner who is ready and has the time to invest in your goals. Not everybody we know is interested in seeing us succeed, and even if they do, they may not have the wherewithal to encourage or push us to go for the goal. Many times, we have been disappointed because we had expectations of certain loved ones to help us achieve our goals and they failed to meet the expectations. You need to find someone or hold on to someone who has not only shown interest in seeing you do well but is also willing to invest in you. You need a partner who is willing and available to check that agreed milestones are reached.

It is okay to have more than one accountability partner. Every person is graced in different areas of life. So, you don't really have to put all your eggs in one basket. When you set out to achieve a goal, all areas of your life are affected, and it is important that you nourish those areas along the journey to maintain a good balance. You may therefore need accountability partners spiritually, emotionally, mentally, and physically. The more partners you have, the less likely it is to slack in reaching your goals.

Hold your accountability partners accountable. Let them know ahead of time that you are counting on them to help keep you on track. If possible, let them know what you are expecting from them and how they can be of assistance. God has placed men (and women) in your life to support you, but if you do not reach out to them, or make yourself accountable or answerable to them, you may be on the journey alone and trust me, this can be very long and lonely.

Lastly and most importantly, know that you are accountable for your own actions. I know this is easier said than done, but you need to learn to encourage yourself more. You need to start taking sole responsibility for your actions. 1 Samuel 30:6 (KJV) says of David," ...But David encouraged himself in the Lord his God." This is what you must learn to do for yourself too. John G. Miller quipped, "Personal accountability is never about others; it's always about me looking in the mirror and making better choices."

CHAPTER 9

HANDLING EXPECTATIONS

"The best things in life are unexpected - because there were no expectations."

- Eli Khamarov

O kay, so let me first give you the good news - people, including your friends and loved ones, are going to disappoint you, even when you are going through adversity. Yes, I say it's good news because once you have that at the back of your mind, you are better prepared in the face of disappointment. The earlier you understand that the world does not owe you, the easier it will be for you to navigate through change.

It's certainly not out of place for you to expect that when you are going through adversity, people who you hold so dear to you will support you through those trying times. The problem is, when we place expectations on others, we set ourselves up for disappointment. You may have had instances in which you were there for a friend or a family member in their time of need, but when the tables turned, they were nowhere to be found, even when you knew they were well able to help.

The reason why a lot of people are frustrated and eventually give up when they go through adversity is that they have too much expectation of someone else to make things better. See, it is good to have expectations - having a support network is fantastic; but the reality is that people will not always be there when you need them.

Often, we tend to believe that the way we treat others will be the way we will be treated in return. But, unfortunately, this does not always happen. We need to learn how to take responsibility for our own lives and our own decisions before we can expect others to do the same.

Expecting life to always turn out the way you want is guaranteed to lead to disappointment because life will not always turn out the way you want it to. This we have established in previous chapters. But when those unfulfilled expectations involve the failure of other people to behave the way you expect them to, the disappointment can also lead to resentment.

One of the biggest challenges we face in life is learning to accept people for who they truly are. Once you realise that your expectations cannot change people, the better off you will be. Problems often arise when expectations do not materialise. If you find that you are going out of your way much more than the people you surround yourself with, it may be time to find a new group of friends. It was the late American poet, Maya Angelou, who said: "People know themselves much better than you do, that's why it's important to stop expecting them to be something other than who they are." Expectation, indeed, is the root of all heartaches.

Antidote to Disappointment

I believe one of the keys to happiness lies within the management of your expectations of people and circumstances. If you do not have expectations, you can never be disappointed.

An unfortunate pitfall of having high expectations in certain circumstances is that we prevent ourselves from enjoying the experience altogether. If you feel this way in your life, you need to readjust your expectations. Do not expect things out of situations; just go into them with an open mind. This will allow you to fully immerse yourself without the pressure of living up to preconceived notions.

When you have unrealistic notions about people, you place yourself at a high risk of getting disappointed and hurt. Maybe someone did let you down on certain occasions, but isn't it inherently unfair to have them on such a pedestal in the first place? By maintaining an accurate awareness of your own realities, you become able to determine what is truly expected from others.

Own Your Journey

Whatever it is that you feel at any point in time is felt by just you, no one else can feel it. You often" hear people say things like, "I can imagine", but truly most times they cannot imagine what you are going through. They are not in your shoes, so cannot tell where it hurts; they can only empathise with the pain. When you are getting ready to have a baby, in the delivery room, you are the one who does the pushing; those aiding in the birth are only cheering you on to PUSH.

Acceptance is an amazing trait that needs to be actively pursued. When things do not work out the way we have planned, it is much more beneficial to realise that is how life works, rather than becoming frustrated about the situation. Have hope rather than expectations and you will tend not to be as disappointed. Expect what you can, reach out but be aware of the fact that sometimes life throws you a curveball. Try to remain confident while maintaining positive aspirations. Just remember not to make these aspirations so high that they are impractical or unreachable.

I understand that we all have different thresholds for handling situations, but we must learn to own our personal journey, and make a blockbuster out of it. Before redundancy came knocking, I had always thought I had it all together, because I take a proactive approach to things. Yes, I do try to fulfil all righteousness. But, frankly, redundancy robbed me of my "mojo" at the time. I got to a point where I was at an all-time low. When your mojo drops to zero level, you are like a bird whose wings have been clipped, and unable to fly. I began to question my ability to do things I would normally do without any stress. I became dejected. I experienced rejection. I was subjected to oppression – yes, even by some loved ones!

Facts versus TRUTH

However, while these are my facts, I have come so far as to know that the facts cannot suppress "the truth". The truth is what the word of God says concerning my situation. The truth informs the company that I keep; the truth informs the words I expose myself to; the truth informs the choices I make; the truth informs the decisions I make.

I understand from the truth that an adverse circumstance does NOT define me. I understand from the truth that I must not allow a phase I'm going through to disable me. I understand from the truth that there are secret opportunities hidden in every setback. I understand from the truth that my life must not be put on hold because of what I am going through. I understand from the truth that I may not be able to control what happens around me, but I am able to CHOOSE how I react.

I understand from the truth that starting over again does not mean starting from the scratch but starting from experience. I understand from the truth that I might not have become a better person if I had not gone through certain experiences. I understand from the truth that I must learn the secrets of keeping my joy in ALL seasons, because my joy is anchored in Christ. Oh, how I understood so many things from the truth!

Quit the Blame Game

Can I shock you? The blame game is one game that you will always lose big time! Man, at his best, will fail you. The best of men are still men, at best. The best people are still human and will have their shortcomings. Just as you do.

While your experiences have a way of revealing who your true friends are, how you handle the situations you find yourself also exposes the real You. Have you met people who always blame everybody for their woes? They blame their parents, spouses, bosses, pastors, church members, siblings, business partners - everybody, except themselves. Excuse me, do you know that you played a part in whatever situation you find yourself in now? And you want to ask what that part is – it is settling! You have settled because of what people did or did not do. You have settled because you have forgotten that God's ways are not our ways, and He is able to meet you at your point of need by using a total stranger. You have settled because you have not realised that there are certain people that God does not want to appear in the honours list of your glory because He alone wants to take all the glory.

You have settled for less because of the negative names somebody else has called you, and you believe you have failed because those words keep ringing in your head. You have settled because you cannot move past your past mistakes as they haunt you. Settling for less than God's best for you is going to keep you bound and prevent you from moving forward.

The Right Approach

So, what should you be doing, instead of settling for negativity or mediocrity – or expecting people to be the ones to rescue you from the clutches of adversity?

- **Forgive yourself**
  Do not let your past trap you, let it make you a better, stronger person.
  Sometimes we think the world should revolve around us, but it is not all about us and our expectations. People are at different levels of awareness and to walk in unconditional love is to allow people to be who they are.
  Steve Maraboli counsels, "Set the standard! Stop expecting others to show you love, acceptance,

commitment, and respect when you don't even show that to yourself."

Let go of expectations and find something to be grateful about, even when things do not turn out the way you hoped - and you will experience serenity rather than resentment.

- **Forgive others**

  Your purpose is too valuable for you to allow unforgiveness to deprive you of what God has in store for you. Release those who have offended you in prayers and let them go if they have no place in your life anymore.

  Give without expectation, accept without reservation, and love without hesitation.

  Psalms 118: 8 says, "It is better to trust in the Lord than to put confidence in man".

  The arm of flesh will fail you.

  Expect the unexpected, believe in the unbelievable, and achieve the unachievable.

"It may not be your fault for being down, but it is your fault for not getting up," says Steve Davis.

CHAPTER 10

CONNECTING THE DOTS

"Dream big. Start small and then connect the dots."

- Dan Millman

The purpose of a thing is the reason for its existence. The purpose of a thing is the creator's original purpose for it. Everything that was designed was designed on purpose, for a purpose and equipped with purpose. The purpose of a thing therefore predates the thing. This means that before you were formed, you had been predestined. You carry a purpose which you were sent into the earth to fulfil. And if you do not understand the purpose of your life, then your life is subject to abuse. As Myles Munroe said, "When purpose is not known, abuse is inevitable."

The only person who can accurately define purpose is the Creator and not the carrier of the purpose. It is imperative therefore that you discover your purpose by aligning with your Creator. Everything you need to fulfil this purpose is already in you. Therefore, when adversity arises, it must always draw you back to the purpose for which you were created.

Proper Perspective

I want you to look at whatever adversity you are facing from a different perspective; see it as a fuel for greatness. You do not have to like it. You will not enjoy it. But what you will need to do is believe in it and embrace the role it's playing in your life in turning you into an embodiment of strength. It is the learning that comes from the adversity that creates opportunity for growth.

I once listened to the speech given by the late Steve Jobs during a graduation ceremony at the prestigious Stanford University. Steve shared his story about love and loss.

Steve had been lucky enough to find what he loved to do early in life. He had started the company, Apple, from his parents' garage when he was 20 years old with his friend. In 10 years, Apple had grown from two people in the garage into a 2 billion-dollar company, with over 4,000 employees. And then he got fired – yes, fired at the age of 30 from the company that he started!

What happened was that, as Apple grew, the management had hired someone who Steve considered very talented to join in running the company. A few years down the line, however, Steve and the individual had a fallout. The board of directors sided with the other partner and Steve was fired. Everything that was the focus of his entire adult life was gone. Steve narrated how devastating that was. He had lost everything he worked so hard for.

Can you imagine yourself in his shoes right now?

But then, according to Steve, something dawned on him. Even though he was being rejected, he was still in love - with his passion. So, he decided to start all over. Within the next five years, he had started two successful companies, one of which went on to become the world's most successful animation studio in the world. In a remarkable turn of events, Apple bought one of his new companies, and Steve was back at Apple again.

In hindsight, Steve realised that getting fired from Apple was the best thing that could have happened to him. The heaviness of being successful was replaced by the lightness of being a beginner again, Steve recalled. It freed him to enter one of the most creative periods of his life. "It was an awful-tasting medicine, but I guess the patient needed it," he said.

As Steve continued to charge the graduating students, he told them to trust that they knew where they were going, and that it's only after they got there that they could then connect the dots. Here is an excerpt from the speech:

"You can't connect the dots looking forward; you can only connect them looking backward. So, you have to trust that the dots will somehow connect in your future. You have to trust in something — your gut, destiny, life, karma, whatever. This approach has never let me down, and it has made all the difference in my life."

Wow. That just goes to show you that for every great and exceptional person you see, there is a story that precedes their glory. They have invested in themselves by being disciplined in their quest to fulfil purpose.

Unleash Your Creativity

Redundancy opened a chance for me to explore my untapped creativity. I would perhaps not have devoted much time to exploring my real passion and fully maximising the purpose for which I was created.

There is creativity within you that you have allowed to lie dormant because of the circumstances around you - situations you have found yourself in and the discouragement you have experienced. The beauty of life is the beauty that you bring to it. As long as this earth remains, seedtime and harvest will never cease. You must give something in order to receive something.

Do not let the weight of regrets, doubts and past glory slow you down, or stop you from arising from that adversity. You can never run with speed if you are carrying a weight. All the circumstances that surround our lives are either a lesson or a blessing.

Perhaps God is taking you through a journey of rediscovery. Do not ditch the process, embrace the journey. With God - the Master Creator - you can rise above any adversity and come out victorious. In fact, once you can conquer the first one, it makes you better prepared to face the next. Yes, you got me right, the next one. Remember, "Many are the afflictions of the righteous..." (Psalm 34:19). In this world, we are constantly engaged in warfare. The choice I want you to make is that adversity will not break you but make you.

Choose to be Resilient

Bear in mind that adversity has seasons and stages. And for every of these stages, God has made a way of escape; all He is asking is that you do your part.

When you find yourself in a crisis, you cannot be quiet about it and wait to see what will happen. You cannot leave things up to somebody else. You must respond as soon as possible by initiating a solution. Take a first step - any step is better than no step.

Regardless of where the wind of life has blown you, stay focused on your dreams and vision. It's never too late to start again but this time you are not starting from the scratch, you are building on past experiences.

Ways to Connect the Dots

- **Review, revise and reset your vision**
  To connect the dots of your life, re-examine your God-given purpose, or what you want to become. Review what you want to do with your life and your desired future. Make it specific, make it clear, make it plain. Habakkuk 2:2-3 says: "Write the vision and make it plain on tablets, that he may run who reads it. For the vision is yet for an appointed time; but at the end it will speak, and it will not lie. Though it tarries, wait for it; because it will surely come, it will not tarry."

- **Assess your obstacles**
  Many people overlook this point. It is particularly important to do a reality check about your situation. Evaluate your present resources which may include physical, material, emotional resources. Also evaluate the resources required for where you are currently headed. Deal with your limiting beliefs by seeking help where required and also harnessing your uplifting beliefs. Be honest about these assessments, then list specific steps that you will take to get back on

course. Philippians 4:8 gives a clue: "...Whatever things are true, whatever things are noble, whatever things are just, whatever things are pure, whatever things are lovely, whatever things are of good report, if there is any virtue and if there is anything praiseworthy - meditate on these things."

- **Cut off relationships that are detrimental to your growth, and change environments that may hinder your progress**

  Truth be told, there are times you may need to sever some relationships to be able to reach your goals. Once you have your mind set to achieve a goal, you need to surround yourself with people who can cheer you on, encourage you or assist you in one form or the other. The same applies to your environment. Ensure you remain in environments that help you focus on your goals. Take necessary steps to free yourself from negative influences and create new positive environments through which you can follow your priorities and experience personal growth. Psalm 1:1-3 says, "Blessed is the man, who walks not in the counsel of the ungodly, Nor stands in the path of sinners, Nor sits in the seat of the scornful; But his delight is in the law of the Lord, And in His law he meditates day and night."

- **Refuse to give up**

  To overcome a crisis, you need to fully commit to finding a way forward. You must approach the problem, determined and motivated. This will create a mindset in which you look at adversity as something to be overcome and solved, not passively accepted.

Sometimes dilemmas and obstacles are a chance to create alternative paths, to dream bigger, to push forward and take even larger leaps.

But whatever you do, you cannot give up. Michael Jordan has famously said, "I've missed more than 9,000 shots in my career. I have lost almost 300 games. On 26 occasions I have been entrusted to take the game winning shot, and I missed. I have failed over and over and over again in my life. And that is why I succeed."

If you refuse to give up, you will always go further than you expected. Galatians 6:9 exhorts, - "And let us not grow weary while doing good, for in due season we shall reap if we do not lose heart".

- **Believe in your capabilities**

  People who rebound from adversity begin by believing they can find a way forward. If you feel hopeless and powerless, it is unlikely you will find a way to be successful.

  You must have self-confidence and a strong belief in your capabilities to overcome difficult times. You must be open-minded and willing to leverage your talent, know-how and ingenuity to overcome adversity.

  If you need more inspiration, consider the story of Walt Disney, who was fired from his first job for not being creative enough. However, Disney never stopped believing in himself and in his dreams. He went on to found what is now the Walt Disney Company, a multinational mass media conglomerate. He once said, "All the adversity I've had in my life, all

my troubles and obstacles, have strengthened me...
You may not realize it when it happens, but a kick in
the teeth may be the best thing in the world for you."
No wonder Paul the Apostle too said, "I can do all
things through Christ who strengthens me"
(Philippians 4:13).

- **Your choices must change your direction**

  Even when you think you are on course, take time out
  periodically to review, renew, revise, and refocus your
  flight path, as necessary. Always stop to ask yourself,
  "Am I going the way I want to go? Am I becoming the
  man or woman that I committed myself to becoming?
  Am I doing things that will change me into the person
  I want to become?"

  The direction you are currently on will affect your
  whole life. If you need to make a correction, take
  courage and do so. Do not let adversity change your
  direction, let your choices lead you on your journey.
  As you travel along that journey, ask God for wisdom.
  James 1:5 assures, "If any of you lacks wisdom, let
  him ask of God, who gives to all liberally and without
  reproach, and it will be given to him."

Arise and Shine!

There's something about winning in the face of adversity.
There's something about resurrecting what has been
declared "dead". There's something about experiencing a
shine after you've had the dullest season of your life. There's
something about that glow that manifests when you get your
groove back. There's power in birthing purpose through your
pain.

Can I encourage you to let that adversity lead you into a place of adventure - the adventure that will ultimately lead you to your desired destiny! Now is the time to respond. Today is the day to act. Today is the beginning of your future. You have the ticket to the next dimension in your hand. Do not resign to fate. Do not settle for less than the best God has for you. You have the power within you to rise and take your rightful place.

I pray that you will truly have an encounter within the adversity that you may be going through, that will change the course of events in your life for the better.

If you ever get to lose anything in life, do not lose the lessons you've learnt from your journey!

Printed in Great Britain
by Amazon